CHAMPION SPORT

B I O G R A P H I E S

TONY HAWK

CHAMPION SPORT
BIOGRAPHIES

TONY HAWK

MICHAEL BOUGHN

Warwick Publishing Inc.
Toronto Chicago
www.warwickgp.com

Champion Sport Biographies
Tony Hawk
© 2001 Maverick Communications

We acknowledge the financial support of the Government of
Canada through the Book Publishing Industry Development
Program for our publishing activities.

ISBN: 1-894622-02-2

Published by **Warwick Publishing Inc.**
162 John Street
Toronto, Ontario M5V 2E5 Canada
www.warwickgp.com

Distributed in the United States by:
LPC Group
1436 West Randolph Street
Chicago, Illinois 60607

Distributed in Canada by:
General Distribution Services Ltd.
325 Humber College Blvd.
Toronto, ON M9W 7C3

Design: Clint Rogerson
Editor: Joseph Romain
Cover and interior photos:
Printed and bound in Canada

Table of Contents

Factsheet

Tony Hawk Stats

Birthday: May 12, 1968
Birthplace: San Diego, California
Hometown: Carlsbad, California
Height: 6'2" / 188 cm
Stance: Goofy
Favorite Food: Taco Bell
Married: wife, Erin
Children: 2 sons, Riley and Spencer
Companies: Birdhouse Enterprises, Fury Trucks, Hawk clothing and shoes.
First year as pro: 1982 (he was 14 years old)
Retired: 1999 (31 years old)

Some of Hawk's moves:

1980: backside varial
1986: backside ollie to tail
1987: backside pop-shove-it
1988: 360 varial to fakie
1989: ollie 540
1990: varial 540
1994: kickflip mctwist
1998: varial 720
1999: 900
2000: frontside stale-fish 540

Introduction

Skateboarding is a funny sport — hardly a sport at all, really, especially if you think of sport as a competitive activity with rules. A better description of skateboarding might be guys (and a few girls) on wheels doing tricks.

That is, if you didn't know any better.

Take Tony Hawk at the 1999 Summer X games. At 31 years old, he was pushing the envelope for skaters. He'd been at it for 25 years, ever since his big brother had given him an old skinny banana board. It was a fiberglass Bahne and Tony was only six years old at the time. In all those years, years in which he had climbed to the heights and sunk to the depths of skateboarding, he'd done just about every trick you could pull on a plank with wheels.

Sometime around the end of the 80's, Tony had made a list of tricks he wanted to do during his career. The list included an ollie 540, a kickflip 540, a varial 720, and topping his list was the 900. Strange-sounding names for dangerous stunts performed at tremendous speeds in the air with no net. By 1999, Tony had managed them all — except the 900, or the "9."

Tony Hawk is a vert skater. The 9 involves flying down a vertical gradient and up the other side. When he becomes airborne at the top of his ride, he has to complete two and half revolutions in the air, then land on his wheels and skate intact off the ramp. No skater had ever done it before — and not for lack of trying.

Tony had been trying for over a decade. The first time, in 1989, he had tried over and over, but eventually had to admit failure. The next time he went at it was while shooting a skateboard video in 1994. The people involved in the film helped Tony build a special ramp to make the trick more possible. But after three days of falling he still hadn't done it. Then after the three days were up, he refused to quit for another seven. By the time he finally admitted defeat he had hurt himself so badly — including a serious back injury — that he couldn't even walk, forget skate, for over a week.

Then came the Summer 1999 X Games. There was a lot of hot skating going on in the Best Trick competition. All the top contenders were there — Bucky Lasek, Bob Burnquist, Andy MacDonald, and Colin McKay. Bucky Lasek was performing heelflip frontside Cabs. Bob Burnquist had pulled off a fakie 5-0 to kickflip. And after only three tries Tony had completed a varial 720 (going up the ramp backwards, spinning two complete revolutions while turning the board 180°, and landing facing forward with the board backward). The energy was high and Tony probably had first place tied up. In some other sports, that would have been enough. But that's not what skating is all about.

With 15 minutes left, Tony decided to give the 50,000-strong crowd something to remember. He decided to shoot for the 9. The first few attempts were close. Tony could feel a difference in the way he was twisting. He was coming around in a way he never quite had before. He almost had it, he felt, and the crowd could tell that too. But he kept missing his landings, pulling off the rotations, only to fall time after time.

The crowd started to go nuts. "Tony, Tony, Tony, Tony," they chanted, filling up the San Francisco sky and rattling the TransAm building blocks away. Even the other skaters stopped skating and fell in behind him at the top of the ramp, urging him on.

"9, 9, 9," the crowd roared. The time for the Best Trick event was well over now, but nobody cared. The excitement of the crowd was electric. It got higher and higher after every one of Tony's attempts, and as it got higher it fed his own single-minded drive to pull off the 9. Later, Tony would write that it would have taken every security guard on the site to haul him off the ramp at that point.

It's almost impossible to think of such a scene happening in any other sport being played today. But then skateboarding is, as they say, in a league of its own. No one knows quite when it started, although everyone agrees it has been around for a long time. Not that it looked, in its early forms, anything like it does today.

Some people say the first skateboard was a scooter with the handle broken off. Others say it was a plank of wood with roller skate wheels nailed to the bottom. Some people say the first skateboard was invented in the 1930's or 40's, or even the early 1900's. Others say it was probably invented right after some cave guys thought up the wheel. In fact, some people think a couple of 14-year-old cave guys may have invented the wheel in order to skate.

Whatever the true story, everybody agrees that it wasn't until the 1950's in California that what became the modern skateboard was invented — 1958, to be exact — and that it grew out of the surfing community. During the 1950's surfing became hugely popular in California. The popularity of the sport wasn't just about the time you were on the board hanging ten, either. It was the whole lifestyle of surfing that was popular.

In fact, surfing may have been the first sport to lay claim to what we now think of as a "lifestyle." Surfing wasn't just about riding waves. It was about spending as much time as possible on the beach. It was about how you cut your hair. It was about what kind of clothes you wore. It was about what kind of car you drove. And most important of all, it was about attitude.

The modern skateboard, the skateboard we know, was created when some surfers got tired of waiting for Mother Nature to whip them up some waves to ride, and left the calmed ocean for a sidewalk. Bill and Mark Richards, a father/son surfer team, came up with the idea and made a deal with a roller skate company in Chicago to supply them with special sets of wheels that they could attached to wooden boards. The new trucks, along with the development of clay wheels, changed everything. The sport soon to be known as "sidewalk surfing" was born.

It was hardly the technical sport we know today, in either its street form or its vert form. Mostly guys just looked for a hill and took off, trying to stay on the board as long as they could. They were carving cut backs, hanging ten, and walking the nose like surfers did, only they were doing it on the asphalt surfaces of urban subdivisions. By 1959 the first Roller Derby Skate Board went on sale. Then rock'n'roll duo Jan and Dean released their single, "Sidewalk Surfin'." It was a huge hit, and before anybody knew what had happened, everybody was sidewalk surfing.

In the early 60's, skating really took off. Larry Stevenson, the publisher of *Surf Guide*, an important surfing magazine, began to promote the sport, even as his company began to produce the first professional boards. Some kids in Hermosa Beach, California, organized the first skateboarding competition in 1963. A hundred people showed up for it. Then in 1964, surf legend Hobie Alter came out with Hobie Skateboards.

Skateboarding made the popular weekly television show, *Wide World of Sports,* for the first time that year when ABC broadcast the National Skateboard Championships. Skating even made the front cover of *Life* magazine. Skating was on a major ride. But it couldn't last much longer. When *Life* described the skateboard as "the most exhilarating and dangerous joy-riding device this side of the hot rod," it didn't take a rocket scientist to figure out that a lot of people (read "adults") were going to want to shut it down as soon as possible.

And in fact, they went on the warpath almost overnight. In a movement led by no less an organization than the American Medical Association (AMA), skateboarding was declared a "new medical menace." Parents everywhere were urged to seize their kids' boards and destroy them. And it worked. Cities started banning boards because of worries about being sued if someone got hurt. Within a year, the skateboarding craze died.

Of course, it wasn't just the AMA that was to blame for the death of the sport. The boards themselves, though way better than the tacked-together boards on roller-skate wheels that preceded them, were still no great shakes. The clay wheels were a problem because they didn't grip the road very well. A lot of skaters were going down just because their boards couldn't hold the road. And that was causing a lot of unnecessary injuries.

Between 1962 and 1965 over 50 million skateboards were sold in the United States. Then almost overnight, the demand for skateboards shrank to nothing. Manufacturers who had been counting on the Christmas season to make money couldn't sell a board if their lives depended on it. Companies dropped like flies. Suddenly, you couldn't buy a skateboard even if you wanted one — and only a few people still wanted them.

However, if skateboarding was down, it was far from out. It may have been the first time the sport died, but it sure wouldn't be the last.

It would be eight years, more or less, before the sport got back on its feet again. During that time it went underground, where a dedicated group of hardcore skaters kept it alive. Two developments in the early 70's led to the rebirth of the sport that Tony Hawk joined and mastered. The first was Larry Stevenson's invention of a "skateboard with inclined foot-depressible level," as the 1971 patent read. Stevenson, of course, had invented the kicktail, an upward curve at the back of the board that permitted far more maneuverability than had ever been possible before.

The other important skateboard innovation around

this time was the urethane wheel. Originally made for indoor roller-skating, these wheels were adapted by Frank Nasworthy for use on a skateboard. The urethane gripped the road better than the old clay wheels, and were lighter. Nasworthy went on to found Cadillac Wheels, and along with the development of better trucks for housing the wheels and the addition of precision bearings, Nasworthy's new wheels helped fuel the rebirth of skateboarding in the mid 1970's.

But this revived skateboarding was unlike anything that had ever been seen before. Within a matter of a few years, guys began pulling off tricks and creating moves that no one would have imagined possible on the old clunky boards. This was the skate world Tony Hawk entered when his older brother passed on his old Bahne board to him in 1974. In 1978 Alan Gelfand changed the sport forever when he pulled off the first ollie, tapping down the kicktail and jumping into the air while his front foot slid forward. Houston, we have lift-off! Other moves followed, like aerials, grinders, fakies, and Rock'n'Rolls, revolutionizing the sport.

Perhaps most important of all, in 1976 the first skatepark dedicated solely to skateboarders was built in Florida. Within a matter of a few years more than 300 skateparks had sprung up across North America. The skateparks fundamentally changed the way skateboarding was done. Before the birth of the skateparks, most skating was done on the street or other level surfaces, and involved slalom and freestyle skating.

The first generation of true skating stars like Tony Alva, Stacy Peralta, Bruce and Brad Logan, Laura Thornhill, Jay Adams, and Wally Inoyoue moved skating from the horizontal plane to the vertical plane. It's not that it hadn't been done before. Even back in the 50's and 60's a few brave souls had tried skating inside empty swimming pools. But now pool skating became hugely popular and the skateparks, built exactly to serve the needs of the new boards, allowed a whole new range of moves in a supportive environment. Skateboarding became so popular that in two years in the late 70's more than 40 million boards were sold in the U.S.

Huge contest sites opened up, too, including the Los Angeles Sports Arena, Jack Murphy's Stadium in San Diego, Catalina Island off the coast of southern California, and Long Beach Arena. Teams from across the U.S. came to these sites to compete against each other for cash prizes in contests such as freestyle, slalom, barrel jump, high jump, and cross country skating.

The other popular mode of skateboarding, street style, started to develop at the same time when skaters took vertical moves and applied them to the street. Perhaps most important of all, this was the time when skating culture blossomed, just as the surfing culture that preceded it had. Graphic designs, especially skulls, appeared on boards. Skaters started wearing a certain kind of clothes, surf-derived "rad-wear," and then baggy pants and oversize shirts. As the skateboard culture joined forces with New Wave music and punk, and later rap, a certain attitude became associated with skating, an outsider attitude. *Thrasher,* skateboarding's newest magazine, which was started in 1981, documented the new and radical attitude.

This attitude would serve hardcore skaters well over the next few years when skating had died its second brutal death. This time it wasn't doctors who did in skating, it was the insurance industry made up of brokers and number crunchers called actuaries. The increasingly extreme nature of the tricks kids were doing led to more and more injuries, and insurance companies responded by jacking up their premiums so high that skateparks couldn't afford them. Almost overnight, the skatepark vanished from the American landscape, falling one by one under the grinding treads of bulldozers.

But, like the first time around, even though most kids abandoned skating in droves, the hardcore went underground. They made their own wooden skateparks wherever they could find space in their neighborhoods. And more and more, they turned to the city itself, re-imagining the spaces and the objects that make it up. For others the city is about getting to work or going shopping. For skaters, the city is about the ride, and everything in it — ledges, walls, hydrants, rails, steps, benches, planters, curbs, banks — are opportunities.

"Skaters can exist on the essentials of what is out there," Stacy Peralta wrote. "Any terrain. For urban skaters the city is the hardware of their trip."

"Find it. Grind it. Leave it behind," became the rallying cry of the urban skater. The world itself looks different to them. They have what *Thrasher* calls the "skater's eye": "Angles, spots, lurkers and cops all dot the landscape that we travel."

Skating came back again of course, in a third miraculous rebirth. It even became more popular than ever before, eventually claiming as many as ten million skaters. That was the wave Tony Hawk rode to fame and fortune and to the top of the ramp in San Francisco at the Summer X Games in 1999. Listening to the crowd chant his name while the breeze from the Bay blew across his face, all that history was probably the last thing in his mind. But it is what got him up there. What got him down — well, that was something else.

"9, 9, 9," the crowd screamed. It was deafening. On his 12th try, Tony took off down the ramp, up and back down, then up again, his body rolling into a ball, twisting, spinning, 1 — 2 — 3, then making the landing, down and through, his board on the bottom. It was unbelievable. He rose up, stunned, a hand raised in victory. He had done it. The first 900 in history! The crowd went wild. His friends charged him, hoisted him into the air, and carried him around. It was an unbelievable moment, and all the more so because of what Tony Hawk later wrote about it: "Skating is not about winning, it's about skating the best you can and mutual appreciation."

Chapter One

Early speculators on the destiny of young Tony Hawk never even considered that he might become the world's best skateboarder. Most of them saw a potential for doing hard time at some maximum-security institution.

On May 12, 1968, Tony Hawk entered the world. Today we would call Tony a "challenging" child, but back in 1968, he was just a spoiled brat.

He was, to say the least, a difficult child, even by his own standards. One of his earliest memories is of ambushing his babysitter with a well-aimed toy truck fired from his playpen. He didn't much care, even when he was three years old, for people having power over him. And he never hesitated to let them know how he felt. The babysitter quit shortly afterwards, unable to deal with his toddler anger.

And it was all downhill from there, so to speak. Partly it may have had to do with the fact that he was the last of four kids — way last. His oldest sister, Lenore, was 21 when Tony was born. Patricia was 18, and his brother Steve was 12. His parents hadn't planned on having a fourth child.

His mom was 43 and his dad was 45 when Tony joined the Hawk clan. That's not so old to be having kids these days, but in 1968 it was pretty unusual. Not very many people in their forties were having kids. Tony's parents weren't out to do anything radical. They figured they were done with babies. Their oldest kids were off to college, leaving only Steve at home. They were starting to kick back and take it easy when the unexpected happened, as it often does. The next thing they knew they were starting all over again.

Luckily for baby Hawk, his parents were pretty laid back. Tony's dad, Frank, was a war hero turned sales-man. He had been a pilot in the U.S. Navy during World War II and the Korean War and had flown many combat missions. He'd won a bunch of medals, includ-ing a Distinguished Flying Cross and a Gold Star. But even all that couldn't quite prepare him for Tony.

Tony's mom, Nancy, was pretty extraordinary too. Five years before Tony was born, she had decided to go back to university, studying at night. She would be in her fifties when she finally earned her Masters degree. And she didn't stop then. She forged ahead and earned a Ph.D. in education when she was 62, maybe to try to figure out what to do with her youngest child.

Tony later felt that his development as a child had a

lot to do with the fact that his parents were older when he was born. "They'd outgrown the strict mom-and-pop rearing and slipped into the grandparent mentality," he wrote in his autobiography. Given that he had a lot of energy as a kid, his parents' response was to roll with it rather than fight it. "I was a hyper, rail-thin geek on a sugar buzz," he later told writer Sean Mortimer. "I think my mom summed it up best when she said 'challenging'."

Tony figured he had it pretty good — until he had to go out and face the cold, hard world. The first chilly blast he encountered went by the name of "Christopher Robin Preschool." From the four-year-old's point of view, it might just as well have been named Alcatraz. Tony Hawk knew almost as soon as he was dragged through its doors that something had to give. There was no way he was going to hang around there. It was either going to be him or the school.

His strategy, in so far as a youngster could have a strategy, was straightforward. It involved clinging to a fence while screaming at the top of his lungs. Day after day Tony's father dragged him into preschool. Day after day Tony attached himself to the fence like a limpet and screamed like a banshee. Day after day it went on and on, until the teachers finally gave up, defeated by a four-year-old. They expelled him, per-haps the first expulsion from preschool in the history of the United States. Victorious, Tony returned home to his mom, having learned, he claimed later, how important it was never to give up.

And that wasn't the only example of his somewhat unusual behavior. When he was six, his mom took him swimming. Tony spent his entire time in the water trying to swim the length of the pool underwater. When he finally realized he wasn't going to be able to do it, he was furious, and nothing his mother did could calm him down.

The next year he went out for Little League baseball. After getting a hit at his first at-bat, he decided it was a game he was going to like. Unfortunately, he wasn't so lucky the second time at bat and struck out. The six-year-old's response was to run away and hide in a cave in a ravine till his father managed to bribe him out with the promise of an ice cream sundae. That was how it was with young Tony. If he couldn't have it all and have it right away, he freaked out and didn't want any part of it.

It wasn't that he didn't like school. Actually he did quite well. He taught himself to read and to add and subtract in kindergarten by watching *Sesame Street*. He continued to get good marks through first and second grades, but Tony had one problem: he couldn't sit still. He felt like he "had ants crawling all over," he said. "I started to perform mini-aerobic workouts at my desk, fidgeting non-stop."

That didn't go over so well with his teachers, no matter how good his grades were. Nobody could figure him out until his mom finally had the school do an IQ test on him. He scored 144, way above normal, and his teacher explained to his parents that Tony's problem was that he had a twelve-year-old brain in an eight-year-old body. Short of removing his brain and transplanting it into a twelve-year-old body (assuming they could find one), there wasn't a lot they could do.

The school suggested bumping him up a grade so he would be more challenged by the work. The only problem with that was that he would have ended up being way younger than the kids in his class — not a great situation when kids are starting to make friends and figure out social relationships. His parents decided that the cure was worse than the disease. Finally, the school tried putting him in advanced classes while keeping him in the first grade. In a fourth-grade reading class, he watched in horror as the teacher whomped an unruly student on the head with a stack of papers. The next day Tony hightailed it back to his first-grade class, begged the teacher to let him in, and settled right down.

The biggest turning point in Tony's life came when he was six. His brother Steve went away to university in Santa Barbara that year. On one of his trips home, Steve was digging around in the garage and he found his old skateboard buried in a pile of junk. It was practically an antique — a skinny, fiberglass Bahne banana board. He decided to give it to his little brother. History was made.

Steve and Tony spent the afternoon fooling around on the board in the alley behind the house. Tony got frustrated because he couldn't make the board turn or stop, so Steve spent some time showing him the basics of skateboarding. It wasn't what one might call love at first sight. Tony didn't go whacko over skating. In the beginning it was just another toy to him, something he would goof around with if he ran out of other stuff to do. Something had clicked, though, and within a few months his attitude started to change.

Even though Tony was only in first grade, some of his friends were fourth graders, and they were into skating. So he started spending time with them, skating around the neighborhood, "falling all over the place." It wasn't something he was crazy about, but already it had started to change him. What really caught his attention was the skatepark they drove by when he and his family went into San Diego: Oasis Skate Park. Once Tony caught sight of it, all he could think about was joining the hundreds of skaters he saw whipping around the pool, the half-pipe, and the snake run. It might have looked like chaos on wheels to anybody else, but to Tony Hawk it looked like heaven. And he knew he had to get down there.

He pulled out all his best tricks to get to the

skatepark, alternately whining, begging, and threatening his parents. But nothing worked. His father tried to distract him by building a ramp on the driveway. That was okay for a while, but it wasn't Oasis.

Tony was in the fifth grade by the time he finally got there. He went one Saturday with a friend and his friend's mom. Once he walked through the door, he knew his life would never be the same. Padded up with rented gear and looking a bit like an American Gladiator, he walked out into the Park and felt the earth move. All around him kids zoomed up and down, carving back and forth, and pulling stunts Tony had never even imagined possible. "I had entered another dimension," he wrote in his autobiography, "and liked it a lot better than the one I was accustomed to." After skating everything in the park, he remembers having felt content for the first time in his life.

Suddenly, he had to go to Oasis all the time. In the beginning his brother, who had graduated from college and was back in town working, took him a few times a week. When Steve got too busy, Tony got his dad to take over. Everybody noticed the difference in Tony. "When he started getting good at skating it changed his personality," his brother Steve said. "He became a different guy; he was calm, he started thinking about other people and became more generous."

Of course some things didn't change, at least not

right away. If Tony didn't do as well as he thought he should, he would still get a little crazy and disappear into his room with his cat, Zorro. But generally, things were much better, if not for Tony, then at least for his parents and the people around him.

Tony skated everywhere, including in the house. And if he couldn't skate — say when he was stuck in school — then he would draw skateboards and pictures of skating. It occupied him completely. Slowly but surely he started adding to his collection of tricks. His first real trick was a rock'n'roll. After that it was airs. Dave Andrech, one of the most famous and highest skaters of the day, skated at Oasis, and he helped Tony get altitude. Tony's biggest problem was his weight. He was such a scrawny little kid that he could barely get going fast enough to pull most tricks.

One result of that was a hidden blessing. Since he couldn't pop high enough to do most tricks, he started ollieing into his airs, something nobody did in those days. The normal style was to grab your board as you went into the trick. It earned Tony a lot of ridicule from other skaters, and for a long time he was embarrassed that he had to do it. In the long term, though, it served it him well. As skateboard tricks started to change in the 80's and 90's, early grabbing no longer worked and Tony found himself way ahead of the game.

The determination that verged on craziness when Tony was younger now poured into his skating. Many was the day when his brother or father would come to pick him up at the park and he would be working on a new trick. Just a minute, he'd say. Just a minute. The minutes would turn into hours before he would finally be dragged away.

But his father stood by him through thick and thin. As Tony got better and better, he started branching out to other skateparks in southern California. His dad was always ready to pack him in the car and take him to some new spot. Later, after Tony started skating in contests, his dad ferried him up and down the California coast. Eventually, Frank Hawk got dissatisfied with the competitive skate organizations that then existed, so he started his own. He founded both the California Amateur Skateboard League and the National Skateboard Association. The NSA would become a particularly important organization in the world of skateboarding. The contests it organized help boost skating to the enormous popularity it enjoyed in the 80's.

Tony started competing when he was 11 years old. He knew skaters were supposed to compete, and so he decided he had to go for it. His first contest was at Oasis. He didn't win anything. In fact it was a disaster. He was so nervous that he blew tricks he had down pat, slamming over and over again. And he was so skinny his pads didn't fit him. Nobody paid any attention to Tony Hawk that day, except maybe to laugh at him. They wouldn't be laughing long. In only a couple of years, the scrawny kid rolling down the half pipe would be the best skater in the world.

Chapter Two

Skateboarding was a bit of a mixed blessing for Tony Hawk when he was a kid. On the one hand, he was an outsider at school, with almost no friends. Even though he always got decent grades, his memories of his school days are mostly of being tormented by jocks or otherwise humiliated. Oasis and later Del Mar skateparks provided him with the only friends he had.

On the other hand, one of the main reasons he was such an outsider was because he was a skater. His hair and clothes were different. And after the popularity of skating collapsed in the early 80's, he insisted on skating when almost everybody else in the world had decided it was about the most uncool thing you could do. In high school, doing something uncool on purpose verges on suicidal. For Tony Hawk, though, there was no choice. Skating was the only thing he was interested in.

Even though he completely blew his first competition, he knew he had to stick with it. He began entering all the competitions he could, researching each skatepark, and planning each performance. He would make lists of all the tricks he was going to do, usually trying to finish with one of his own invention. After a year of competing, Tony was doing well enough to make the Oasis Park team. He was nearly 12 years old, and skating was his life.

It was quite a shock to Tony, then, when at the end of 1980, skating died practically overnight. Skating was changing radically. More and more, freestyle skating was being replaced by the technical — and dangerous — tricks of vert skating. Along with the more radical tricks went more injuries to skaters. And along with more injuries went higher and higher insurance premiums for skatepark owners. As a result, almost overnight, the majority of skateparks in the U.S. simply closed down. The bulldozers and dump trucks moved in, tore them up, and hauled them away. They not only hauled the ruins of the parks away, they hauled the popularity of skating away too. Before Tony Hawk knew what was what happening, he found himself in love with a sport that barely existed.

That was the year Tony got his first official sponsor when Dogtown, a skateboard company, picked him up. They gave him a free board and set of trucks. Unfortunately, the sponsorship didn't last long. The death of the skateparks and the decline in the popularity of skating was taking its toll. The Association of Skatepark Owners (ASPO), one of the primary sponsors of skating competitions, went down for the count. It's hard to have an active association of skatepark owners when there aren't any skateparks. At about the same time, Dogtown seemed to be suffering a terminal illness as well.

Tony's dad, Frank, stepped in to help out with the ASPO problem. Frank Hawk was always strongly supportive of his children's undertakings, whatever they were. In 1981, recognizing that ASPO was not long for this world, Frank organized an alternative skate association, the California Amateur Skateboard League. Immediately, CASL began to organize its own competitions.

When his parents decided to move to a house that was only five minutes from Del Mar Skatepark, Tony was happy. It wasn't that he didn't love Oasis. But no one was skating there anymore. He had the place to himself, and it didn't feel good. Del Mar, on the other hand, still boasted a full and active group of skaters, so Tony was content to shift his allegiance there.

At the same time, Tony was starting to do much better in the competitions. In 1981, with ASPO on its last legs, he took first place at Del Mar in the ASPO Boys 13-14 Division. He did it again in 1982, taking first in four separate competitions. While things were looking better for the 12-year-old, there was a problem. All of his firsts were at Del Mar, which was now his home base. Elsewhere he was placing tenth (Kona) or sixth (Whittier). It was beginning to look like the only place Tony could win was in his own backyard.

By December 1981, things were going badly for Dogtown, Tony's sponsor. Although Tony didn't know it, the company was about to go out of business, unable to withstand the collapse of skating. At the same time, Tony had caught the eye of a couple of other skate companies. G & S and Powell & Peralta were both interested in the young skater. Tony had been scouted by no less a person than the legendary Stacy Peralta. Meanwhile, G & S had sent Tony a deck and wheels, hoping to interest him in skating for them.

The day that Dogtown died, Peralta called Tony up and invited him to come skate at Marina. It was a few months before his thirteenth birthday. Tony was only too happy to take Peralta up on his invitation. It never occurred to him that it might be an audition for the Powell team or that it might be a turning point in his life — which was probably a good thing, otherwise he might have been stressed out. Instead, Tony was relaxed and easy that afternoon, and among other tricks, pulled off a backside air. Peralta, duly impressed by the young skater's determination and flair, offered him a place as the youngest member of the Powell team, the Bones Brigade.

It was quite a team. Tony found himself skating with some of the best skaters in the world, including Steve

Caballero and Mike McGill. Only 18 years old, Caballero had invented one of the most revolutionary moves in contemporary skating, the Caballerial. Still only 12 himself, Tony was both intimidated and star struck. He wanted the older guys to like him so much that one night in the hot tub at Stacy Peralta's place, he actually ate gum from between Caballero's toes, thinking that would impress him and McGill.

It wasn't easy going for Tony in other ways as well. As much as he wanted to impress the rest of his team with his skating skills, he couldn't seem to pull it off. For the first time he found himself skating with a whole new range of skaters. It was the big time, now. Rather than the amateurs from California he was used to, Tony found himself going up against skaters from all over the country. Their skill level, not to mention their confidence level, was higher than anything in Tony's experience. The more stressed out he got, the worse he skated. And the worse he skated, the worse he felt about himself and the more stressed out he got. It was a vicious circle, and Tony Hawk was caught like a hamster, going around and around.

Luckily for him, Stacy Peralta was patient and understanding. He knew how young Tony was and didn't put any pressure on him to win. He figured it would take a while for the young skater to find his legs. It wasn't necessary for him to put pressure on Tony anyway, since Tony was quite capable of putting pressure on himself. Gradually he began to get his confidence back and to win some competitions. He was helped by the fact that in 1982 many of the other top amateurs decided to turn pro. Chris Miller, Neil Blender, and Billy Ruff all went pro that year, leaving Tony pretty much alone at the top of the amateur heap.

That's when Peralta started pushing the 14-year-old to go pro. Tony wasn't crazy about the idea. Pro skaters in 1982 didn't make much money — maybe $150 for first place, if you were lucky. So it didn't seem to the young skater that there was much advantage in it. Still Peralta kept after him, and finally, in 1982, Tony Hawk checked off the pro box on his registration form for a competition at Whittier. He was now officially a professional skateboarder.

Whatever difference that made in Tony's skating life, it didn't make much difference to the rest of his life, which seemed to him pretty unhappy. His days at Serra High School were one long misery after another, mostly having to do with being a total outsider. He was still small for his age, and his skater ways made him stand out from the herd of jocks who ruled the hallways at Serra. Constantly the butt of jokes and rude comments, Tony hoped desperately to get out of Serra. It meant he skated harder and spent even more time at Del Mar.

His wish came true that summer when his parents

decided to move to Cardiff, California. It meant that Tony, finally liberated from Serra, would be doing ninth grade at San Dieguito High School. He was excited about the change in the beginning. But it wasn't long before he realized he'd jumped from the frying pan into the fire. Rather than being better than Serra, San Dieguito was even worse for the 14-year-old. It was if the Serra jocks had all been cloned — only with their mean genes made meaner and their dumb genes made dumber — and moved en masse to San Dieguito.

Part of the problem was that Tony himself was changing in ways that made him stand out even more from the herd — the worst possible thing you can do in high school. The skate scene was developing in new directions, getting more and more involved with punk and New Wave music and styles. Tony bleached his hair and let his bangs hang down over his eyes, and started wearing baggy shorts that went down below his knees. Worst of all, he never tried to hide his involvement with skating, a sport that in the early 80s had a reputation on par with grave robbing.

It wasn't just his fellow students who gave Tony a hard time, either. Skateboarding had a bad reputation, and at San Dieguito, the school responded by banning boards on school property. Tony found one other skater in the school — Miki Vuckovich. They would skate to and from school every day, but they had to be careful, because if the teachers saw them even standing on a board, they would confiscate it.

Tony's size was still causing him problems with his skating. "I was worried," Stacy Peralta said about the 14-year-old Tony. "He was so scrawny that I thought he'd hurt himself. I had to look away sometimes because it was so painful to watch. He put his body through so much punishment." The biggest problem for Tony was getting up enough speed. He weighed so little that it was extremely hard for him to build up the momentum he needed to pull off the tricks. Still, he couldn't have been doing *that* badly: He made the cover of *Thrasher* magazine.

There was no question that whatever the difficulties Tony was having at school, he was definitely coming into his own as a skater. His second pro contest was at Del Mar, a skatepark he knew like the back of his hand. Duane Peters was also skating in the competition. Peters was an older, old-style skater who, a few years earlier, had put Tony down hard when the younger skater had tried to make friends with him.

Peters had a lot of power as he carved through old-time tricks like lay back grinds. But the young Tony had developed an entirely different style, ollieing into his airs, flipping his boards, pushing skating toward a form of gymnastics. In fact he was known as the Circus Skater for all the strange tricks he pulled, many of which he invented himself. Peters couldn't even begin to keep up. When Tony won first place, it was a sign of the enormous changes taking place in skating itself.

Still, outside Del Mar, Tony wasn't doing that well. He placed tenth in his third pro event in Jacksonville, Florida. He placed a meager sixth at the Whittier, California, Christmas Classic. Things started to change, though, when he finally decided he had to bust out of San Dieguito High School. After half a year, he didn't think he could take it anymore. Luckily for him, he lived right on the border between two schools. He found out that if the principal at the neighboring high school, Torrey Pines, would let him, he could switch.

The scene at Torrey Pines was completely different from San Dieguito. They had physical education classes in surfing, and the principal, it turned out, was a very cool guy. He met with Tony and not only did he not get uptight about his skating, he actually approved of it. He decided to let Tony into the school the following fall. It was a huge weight off Tony's shoulders.

Other changes were taking place, too. In 1983 Frank Hawk organized another skating organization, this time a national one. The National Skating Association was the first skating organization in the world to have the support of all the major skateboard companies. The NSA unified the ranking system for skaters and began to organize competitions all over the country.

For Tony, the results were much more concrete. His father's involvement with NSA was hands-on, and among other things that meant housing skaters who came to town for competitions. Sometimes up to 20 skaters would be stashed in various parts of the Hawk house, including the bathtub, the garage, and closets. "Our house looked like a skater bomb had exploded," Tony laughed.

But it wasn't all good times, either. Just at the time when Tony was starting to come into his own as a skater, suddenly he found his world invaded by his parents. Because Frank Hawk was head of the NSA, he was at most of the competitions. Early on there were shortages of help, so Frank recruited Tony's mom to come along and help keep score. For Tony that meant that he had to share his most private and personal world with his parents. That wouldn't be a particularly pleasing fact for most 15-year-olds, and Tony Hawk was no exception.

One thing Tony got that year that most 15-year-olds never get was a skateboard with his own name and graphic on it. Stacy Peralta decided that Tony was becoming well-known enough that Powell & Peralta could make some money off a Tony Hawk skateboard. Peralta asked Tony to suggest a graphic for the board. Tony went to a friend of his who drew and asked him to come up with an image of a swooping hawk. The result was a bit rough — not exactly what Tony had in mind, but he sent it to Peralta anyway. Tony looked at it as a rough draft and figured the Powell artists would polish it up before they put it on a board. Unfortunately he was wrong. When Powell sent him the board, the hawk had been reproduced exactly as he had sent it to them.

It wouldn't have been such a big deal, except that one of the main sources of income for skaters in those days was royalties from the boards. Skaters didn't get money from clothing manufacturers or shoe companies. In 1983, Tony was supposed to get 85 cents per board sold. After a couple of months Tony got his first check. It was for a whopping 85 cents.

The summer of 1983 was a busy one for Tony. Once school was out, he shipped out with the Bones Brigade team. They skated in demos all over Europe, Australia, Canada and the U.S. Tony was beginning to attract a lot of attention. Coming up was a national competition in St. Petersburg, Florida. Tony was tired of hearing how he could only win at Del Mar, so he put a lot of time into getting ready for the St. Petersburg contest. He put together a lot of tricks, including some nobody else could do. They included one-footed inverts and Madonnas.

All the work paid off. When the dust settled, Tony Hawk, professional skateboarder, had won his first pro contest. Nobody could argue anymore that he didn't have what it took to be champion.

Chapter Three

By 1983, the popularity of skating had started to climb again. Nobody knows why skateboarding seems to go through 10-year cycles of popularity, but it does. For Tony, it meant larger and larger crowds at the competitions. And it meant a bit more success making money with Powell & Peralta. After the less than exciting sales of Tony's first deck, Stacy Peralta decided to try again, using a Powell-generated image this time rather than Tony's homemade hawk. The swooping hawk was replaced on Tony's new board by a screaming hawk skull with an iron cross behind it.

The new board became hugely popular, all the more so because of the release of Peralta's first skate video, *The Bones Brigade Video Show*. Stacy had a talent with video that later led him to a career directing films in Hollywood. In 1983, there were no skate videos. It was a revolutionary idea at a time when few people even owned VCRs. *The Bones Brigade Video* was vaguely anti-establishment with lots of skate action and great tricks juiced up by Peralta's surrealistic style. Tony Hawk was featured prominently in the video.

The Bones Brigade Video Show was extremely popular. As a result of the new board and the video, Tony's royalties went up to $3,000 a month — not bad money for a 15-year-old kid in 1983.

As good as Tony was, he was unhappy with his skating. He felt that he still wasn't skating consistently. He was placing all over the map at various competitions. He came in first at the Spring Nationals Pro Am, then fifteenth at the Oceanside Freestyle. He came in first at the Summer World Series but sixth at the Kona Summer Nationals. It was driving Tony crazy, and he couldn't help wondering when Peralta was going to finally give up on him and kick him off the team.

In 1983, Mike McGill stunned the skating world during a competition at Del Mar when he pulled off the first public 540 McTwist. The 540 involves one and a half complete rotations while flipping. The skater goes up the ramp, grabs the board, spins and flips so that he comes back onto the ramp facing forward. It was a completely new kind of trick. McGill worked it out while he was running a skate camp in Sweden. Vertical skating was never the same afterwards.

Every vert skater in the world suddenly had to learn the 540. Tony was no exception. He became completely obsessed with it. It didn't matter where he was, all he could think about was pulling off the trick. He'd run it down in his imagination over and over —

how to pull off the wall, how to flip. But once he actually got on the ramp, he'd chicken out and slam. It was driving him crazy. He couldn't concentrate on his school work. For two months he worked on it, until finally he pulled it off.

Later, Tony made fun of his first successful 540: "I landed the stinkiest 540 you have ever seen in your life," he said. "I squatted like a frog." But he pulled it off. That's all that mattered. At a time when skating was beginning to move in a new direction with a whole new generation of tricks, Tony knew he was still on the wave. Ten years later, the same drive and determination would help him land a heelflip varial at a time when skating was going through a similar crisis and change of direction.

When the end of the year rolled around, it was the time for the NSA to give out its first annual World Champion award. The award was based on the total number of points a skater earned over the course of the year. Tony hadn't been too happy with his consistency since he had joined the Bones Brigade. And he always worried about what others called his "robot style." But regardless of how he felt about himself, others seemed to think he was a pretty good skater. When all the math was done, the NSA declared 16-year-old Tony Hawk to be the best skater in the world.

Tony started off 1984 on a roll. He won the Booney Ramp after falling backward off the top of the ramp and almost breaking his neck. And he placed second at Del Mar — a mixed blessing. He didn't win, but at least he discredited the rumors that said he only skated well at Del Mar. In fact, the more he skated away from his home park, the more comfortable he got. And the more comfortable he got, the better he got. That summer, he went back to Kona Skate Park for the third time as a professional. This time he placed first.

He spent most of the summer just skating around Del Mar, working out new little tricks that he could bring to competitions. He went to San Francisco for a street contest and won it. He skated the Upland Turkey Shoot for the second time. It took place at the Upland Pipeline. The Pipeline was such a difficult run that it was nicknamed the Badlands. In 1983, Tony had come in fourth at the Badlands. In 1984, he almost won. It was a great moment for him because he knew he had given it his best shot and he could feel himself improving as a skater. Others agreed: By the end of 1984, the NSA had awarded the world championship to Tony Hawk for the second time.

Physically, Tony was growing up and it was making a big difference in his skating. In 1985, he measured six feet tall (183 centimetres) and weighed in at 135 pounds (61 kilograms). Not exactly a heavyweight, but the increase in his body mass meant it was getting easier and easier for Tony to build up momentum on the ramp. It showed in his skating, too.

First of all he went back to Del Mar and took first place. And then he went back to the Badlands. This year he was determined to win it. It wasn't going to be easy. The contest was full of locals who knew the difficult skatepark like the back of their hands. Tony's determination drove him, though. He skated harder than he had ever skated in his life. Later he called it "the most important contest" of his career. Winning the Badlands meant proving to all his critics that he wasn't just a circus skater, that he was in it to win. And he did. It was a huge victory for him.

With two consecutive wins under his belt, he next went to Virginia Beach, Virginia, to skate Mt. Trashmore, a ramp built on an old city dump. Mt. Trashmore was important to Tony for a couple of reasons. First of all, when he won the contest, he became the first professional skater to win three consecutive competitions. It may not seem like an earthshaking development, but it was another first for him. But maybe even more important than that, he met a girl.

It's not that Tony Hawk hadn't met girls before. He was 17 years old. But frankly, it wasn't all that easy. Being a skater during all those years when skating was about as popular as the plague certainly didn't help. Most girls in high school took one look at him and thought, "Loser!" There may even have been girls at Serra or San Dieguito or Torrey Pines who liked skaters. But Tony was so busy skating, he might not have noticed. Whatever the reason, he hadn't had what you'd call a busy dating schedule.

Of course there were moments. Once when he was 15 he'd gone to Japan to appear on a TV show called *Miracle Children of the World.* He was put up in a hotel, and just down the hall was a family whose children (mostly girls) were also on the show because of their singing abilities. Much to Tony's surprise, one of those girls lured him into their room that night where she made out with him mere feet away from the girl's snoring parents.

In 1984 Tony had started dating a new girl who worked at the refreshment stand at Del Mar. Sandy lived in the trailer park next to the skatepark. She and Tony had a stormy on again/off again relationship that went on for a long time. When he was competing in Virginia Beach, his relationship with Sandy was in its "off again" mode. Because of his triple win, he was now known as the top vert skater in the world, which meant, among other things, automatic sex appeal. That night he found himself dining out with a beautiful girl he'd met at the competition. After dinner, they went back to his room. In his career as a skater, Tony had done a lot of things he'd never done before. That night, he added one more to the list.

But that wasn't the only important thing that had to

do with girls to happen to Tony that year. In October he went upstate to Fresno, California, for a weekend demo. While he was there, he met a local girl named Cindy Dunbar. They hung around together for the weekend, and even though they didn't even hold hands, they hit it off with each other. As a result, they kept in touch, writing each other letters and developing their friendship over the next few years. Neither of them realized at the time that they'd end up getting married one day.

Tony wound up his junior year of high school still holding a B average. As soon as school was out, he, Rodney Mullen, and Lance Mountain took off for Sweden where they taught at a skate camp for the summer. Needless to say, they managed to get themselves in some trouble. Bored by their enforced confinement at the camp, Tony bought an old Peugeot 404 (one of the best cars ever built, by the way) so they could get away. Actually, they ended up using it as a kind of oversized, enclosed, off-road skateboard, careening down mountains through the woods around the camp.

One day they spotted some pretty girls on a beach and chased them with the car. Pulling donuts on the sand, they were having a great time. Even the girls were amused for a while. But the local police weren't. They tracked the crazy Americans back to the skate camp and were ready to haul them off to jail. The only thing that saved the skaters from doing Swedish time was the police finding out they were from California. Figuring everybody chased each other around the beach in cars in California, the Swedish cops let the three skaters off with a warning that things weren't done like that in Sweden. So instead of chasing girls around in their spare time that summer, Tony, Rodney, and Lance worked on learning 720s.

Tony polished off 1985 with his third NSA World Championship and another Stacy Peralta skate video. Skating became more and more popular with every passing day. This time around, part of that popularity was tied up with a new development — street skating. Street skating combined some of the moves of free style and vert on flatland. The invention of the ollie by Alan "Ollie" Gelfand in 1978 had set the stage for street style by allowing flatland skaters to get airborne. As the new style developed, a new attitude began to develop as well. Peralta's new video, *Future Primitive*, exploited those changes. It began with a statement that defined the essence of street skating and the new attitude: "Two hundred years of American technology has unwittingly created a massive cement playground. It took the minds of twelve-year-olds to realize its potential."

Peralta's video, which included shots of pool skating and some contests — including Tony at Mt. Trashmore — focused on the Bones Brigade skating the streets of San Francisco and Los Angeles. The video was extremely popular. It not only boosted the popularity of Tony and the rest of the Bones Brigade, it helped boost skating as a whole. Tony started getting fan letters from skaters, and his board royalties shot up to $7,000 a month.

More important for Tony, though, was what Stacy Peralta told him. Tony had worked out a whole list of tricks that nobody, including Peralta, had seen before. Tony hadn't performed them in contests because he still wasn't sure enough of himself. While they were shooting the video, Tony spent a morning doing his tricks for Peralta. Afterwards, Tony was worried about what Peralta would say. He needn't have been. "You have the talent to win any contest you want from now on," Peralta told the younger skater. For Tony it was a wonderful moment that built up his self-confidence and left him wanting to keep doing better.

And that's what he did. He didn't need the third NSA championship in as many years to tell him he was one of the most successful and popular skaters in the world. His fans told him that. And there were a lot of them. Skating had come back with a vengeance. Millions and millions of kids took it up. Tony was bombarded with requests for demos and endorsements. He even did a commercial for Mountain Dew that added to his fame. Partly because he was so in demand, his grades started to fall. Luckily for him, his teachers at Torrey Pines were understanding and did what they could to help him make it through his senior year.

Making matters even harder for Tony, his parents moved again. Their new house was outside the Torrey Pines school district. That wasn't such a problem in itself, since Tony was already enrolled there. But it meant he had to become a commuter. He ended up spending 30 to 40 minutes driving each way. It was just one more aggravation he didn't need in his busy life.

He had another problem, too. Well, sort of a problem. He was 17 years old, he was earning $70,000 a year, and he had $50,000 in the bank. That wasn't the problem. The problem was he was paying way too much in taxes on his income. His sister Pat, who did his taxes for him, told him that she thought he should buy a house since then he could deduct his mortgage interest. He could also live closer to school.

Tony liked the idea, so he started shopping around for a house. He finally found a place he liked in Carlsbad. It had four bedrooms and two and a half bathrooms. That suited him fine, since he figured he could get some friends to move in with him. He may have been the only 17-year-old in the U.S. in 1986 to plop down $124,000 for his own house. He was certainly the only one at Torrey Pines High School. Or at Del Mar Skatepark. A couple of friends moved in and Tony's house became skate party central.

He graduated from Torrey Pines that June and threw a major graduation party at his new house. Maybe even an historic graduation party. It was like one of those "Animal House" movies. Cars lined the street. Hundreds of kids boiled in and out of the house. Tony ended up spending the night in a closet with a girl. When they woke up in the morning and climbed out of the closet, they found themselves in what looked like the aftermath of the battle of Waterloo. Picking his way through the sleeping bodies that lay sprawled on the floor and all over the furniture, Tony walked out of the house into the morning of his new life.

Tony mid-revolution in a 540 tail grab.

Tony performs a difficult move — the backside one-footed aerial.

Not only is Tony a great vert skater, he is known for his awesome
street skating abilities. At the Powell indoor skate park he performs
an ollie nose blunt.

Tony pulls an air to fakie on his backyard ramp.

Chapter Four

That summer Tony and the rest of the Bones Brigade went off on a tour around the U.S. It was exhausting, but Tony handled it. He called it five weeks of girls, skating, and parties. The Bones Brigade also shot their third video that summer. *The Search for Animal Chin* was another of Stacy Peralta's slightly surrealistic, action-packed productions, and Tony and the rest of the Bones Brigade had a great time filming it. A special vert spine ramp was built in the country outside Oceanside for most of the ramp skating. Other sequences involved trips to San Francisco, Los Angeles, Las Vegas, and Hawaii. The video emphasized the fun of skating at a time when skating was becoming more and more competitive and focused on winning and making money. It was a change that most hardcore skaters were unhappy with, and Peralta wanted to use his video to make a statement.

As much fun as the summer was, though, Tony returned to Carlsbad to sad news: Del Mar Skatepark was shutting down. The park owners simply weren't able to make enough money to keep it going, especially with rising insurance costs. For Tony it was the end of an era. Although he had first started skating at Oasis, he had spent so much time at Del Mar and was so close to the other skaters there that it was like his second home. He and the rest of the Del Mar gang shifted their skating to the backyard ramp of a friend in Fallbrook. But even though they still skated together, everybody agreed that something was lost when Del Mar closed.

Meanwhile, Tony's career got a huge boost when, in the middle of filming *The Search for Animal Chin*, he went up to Vancouver, British Columbia, and skated a big contest on the Expo '86 grounds. The renewed popularity of skating in Canada meant that the place was packed with appreciative fans. Tony got tagged "the Wayne Gretzky of skating," and *Sports Illustrated* magazine did a big spread on him.

Things were not easy for Tony, however, although looking at his life from the outside, you might have been hard pressed to say exactly why. On the one hand, he seemed to have it made. After cleaning up another NSA world championship award, he was doing well. The popularity of skating continued to grow until it was almost unreal. Contests that might have drawn a few dozen people a couple of years before now packed in 20,000 cheering fans. Tony Hawk was riding that wave. *The Search for Animal Chin* opened in May of 1987 to rave reviews, further spreading his reputation as the world's best skater.

All that translated into big money. Tony's board alone was bringing in royalty checks of $15,000 a month. Add to that the various other royalties from clothing and shoes, and he was doing pretty good for a 19-year-old.

Somehow, though, he couldn't translate his material success into self-confidence and happiness. Of course, when you're at the top, there are always a lot of people trying to bring you down. Critics still complained that Tony had a robot style, and although nobody would say it to his face, he knew. Even worse though, he started to seriously burn out on skating contests. The pressure on him to win and keep winning got more and more intense. It got to the point where if he didn't take first place, everybody thought that he was all washed up. The fun was fast disappearing, and in its place was a kind of mind-numbing demand to win.

One of the worst events during this time for Tony was a demo in Brazil. Four thousand fans came to see the famous Tony Hawk skate. Unfortunately, he got an acute case of food poisoning that went on for a couple of days. He could barely walk, forget skate. The promoter was put out because he was depending on Tony to satisfy the fans. Lacking all sympathy, he forced Tony himself to go to the stadium and announce that he was too sick to skate. After trying unsuccessfully to make the guy understand that he could barely walk, Tony gave in and dragged himself to the stadium. The fans weren't very understanding and he had to listen to four thousand people swear at him in Portuguese while he tried to explain to them how sick he was.

Tony eventually got to the point where he couldn't take it anymore. He wasn't having fun. He was stressed out all the time. He was depressed. And he couldn't figure out why he was still competing. He wanted to quit, but he was worried about what Stacy Peralta would say. Tony was the main earner for Powell, and if he left the Bones Brigade, the company would take a big hit in its earnings.

Tony had a long talk with his brother Steve, and finally decided that he had to retire from competitive skating. He just couldn't do it anymore. He would have to face Stacy Peralta and tell him the truth.

Steve and Tony drove to Stacy's house. Tony was incredibly nervous. He could barely talk when he finally got there. But he knew what he had to do. He forced himself to tell Peralta how depressed and unhappy he was, and how he wanted to retire.

All Tony's worrying was for nothing. Peralta totally understood. He backed Tony all the way. In fact, he wrote him a long letter, telling him what a great skater he was and praising his inner strength. Peralta told Tony that it was a time for him to "take stock and reevaluate" and that he needed to give himself the time to figure out what he really wanted. So at 19 years of age, Tony Hawk won his fourth NSA championship and retired from professional skating. And as if that wasn't enough change for him, in March 1987, he asked Cindy Dunbar to move in with him, too.

The first thing Tony decided to do was take three months off from all skating activity. He really needed a total break, he figured. The second thing he decided to do was buy another house. During his drives out to Fallbrook to skate, he had noticed a place for sale. He now wanted to build his own ramp, and this house, he found out, was sitting on four acres of land. It was perfect.

While he waited for the house deal to close, Tony got involved in making a movie. *Gleaming the Cube* was a film about a skateboarder who avenges his brother's murder. Stacy Peralta was involved in directing the skating sequences in the movie and he hired a bunch of his friends (who happened to be some of the best skaters in the world) to be in the movie. Tony actually got a speaking role as a Pizza Hut delivery boy. But that wasn't his only job on the film. The movie starred Christian Slater, and Tony got to teach him how to skate.

At the beginning of 1988, the house deal closed and Tony and Cindy moved into their new place. The first order of business for Tony was building the ramp.

After all, that's why he had bought the place. He got his dad out there, and together they spent a month designing the ideal ramp. Tony's dad was quite an accomplished handyman. In fact, his kids used to joke that his home away from home was the Home Depot hardware store. So after they figured out what Tony wanted and how they were going to put it together, father and son got down to the business of building it.

While not quite on the scale of the Great Pyramids at Giza in Egypt, Tony's ramp was pretty monumental for a home-made, backyard playground. Of course, how many people have a four-acre backyard with a hill in the middle of it? When the ramp was finished it had three separate sections. The mini-ramp was seven feet high (213 cm) with a spine. Then on top of the hill, they built a 40-foot-wide (12.2-m), 12.5-foot-high (3.8-m) spine ramp, which they connected to a seven-foot-deep (213 cm) bowl.

By the time they were finished, they had used hundreds of 2 x 4s and a 10-foot-high (3-m) stack of plywood. Altogether it cost them $30,000. Stacy Peralta kicked in $10,000 and Tony agreed to let him use the ramp in his next skate video, *Ban This*. Tony had a bit of trouble from one of his neighbors who objected to the ramp, but they got over that. It was the perfect situation for Tony and made the closing of Del Mar easier to bear now that he had a skatepark right in his own backyard.

Taking a three-month vacation from skating paid off for Tony. By the middle of 1988, he was feeling more relaxed than he had in a long time. He changed his mind about retiring and started competing again. Skating had never been more popular, and that summer on the Powell tour, they were pulling in crowds of over 4,000 fans. When the Bones Brigade went to do demos at malls, the police had to protect them from the fans that packed the parking lots. They were even turning down demos because the sponsors didn't have enough room to accommodate the crowds.

At the end of 1988, Tony got involved in another movie when he got a gig as a stunt double for comic actor David Spade. Stacy Peralta was doing more and more Hollywood work, and he got the job directing *Police Academy 4.* He needed some people to do some street skating scenes, and of course he thought of the Bones Brigade. The problem for Tony was nobody thought to check and see whether he and Spade were the same size. After he got on the set, somebody noticed that he was quite a bit taller than the star, and so he got fired. He still got to do the street skating scenes though, which added $5,000 to the $100,000 he earned in 1988.

In 1989 Tony Hawk found himself caught up in some of the huge changes taking place in skating. Those changes had been going on since the 80's when street skating burst onto the scene. Street style was a combination of freestyle and vert moves applied to the street. It moved skating out of the protected environment of the skatepark and onto the streets. In the process the entire city was converted into a series of obstacles for the skater. Since many good citizens objected to kids with funny-colored hair grinding rails and curbs outside their stores, it also increased the conflict between skaters and the police, and intensified skating's rebel image.

Tony Hawk had always been willing to try anything new, and throughout the 80's he had participated in street contests as well as vert contests, even winning some. Vert skating, however, always remained his true strength and his real passion. By the end of the 80's street skating started to overtake vert skating in popularity. One result of that was the birth of new-style skate companies. In 1988, Steve Rocco and Rodney Mullen started World Industries. Then Tony Magnusson started H-Street. While the big, established companies like Powell prided themselves on their straight, clean-cut images, the new small companies knew that the growing popularity of street style was going to radically change the industry.

Street skaters saw themselves as more anti-establishment and outlaw than other skaters. The new companies catered to that image, providing boards and gear that enhanced the rebel image. At the same time they completely undermined the system that had long governed skating. Rather than making amateurs wait a long time and work their way up to the professional level, the new companies put together teams made up of young, crazy skaters with no experience as amateurs. A whole new style took over skating from top to bottom, and the old corporate companies just couldn't keep up with the changes.

A lot of negative elements went along with the new situation in skating. Before, skating was mostly about skating. People did it because they loved it, not because they were driven to win. In the same way, there was a lot of solidarity among skaters, regardless of how old they were or how they skated or what team they rode for. Part of the attitude that the new companies brought with them was an "us vs. them" mentality that applied equally to cops and to other skate teams. There weren't just skaters anymore — now they were divided into "cool" skaters and "uncool" skaters.

Tony was bummed out by these changes. He got even more bummed out when he popped his knee during a demo in Japan. When he got back to the U.S. he had a special scan, called an MRI, done on his knee. The doctors discovered that he'd torn the cartilage in his knee and that it was getting stuck under his knee cap. Every once in a while, his knee would get bent and he wouldn't be able to straighten it. The doctors told Tony he would have to have an operation. As much as he dreaded it, Tony decided to go ahead with the surgery since his knee seemed to be getting worse. After skating on the knee in Hawaii, he couldn't quite get it totally straight again.

The operation wasn't bad. It only took a couple of hours and Tony went home the same day. Barry Zaritsky, the head trainer at NSA contests, moved into Tony's house with him to help him recover. After a few weeks of healthy food and careful exercise, Tony was able to ride a bike. But by the time he was finally healed up enough to skate again, four months had passed.

Tony was determined to get back into the game, though, and pushed himself back into competition. After a second-place in Orange County, he went on to win two contests in Denmark — a vert contest and a street contest — and then another first for vert in Germany. Clearly he was still in the game. He finished up the decade with yet another NSA championship and an income of $150,000 for the year.

Tony Hawk was on top of the world as 1990 began. He was arguably the most famous skateboarder in the world, if not the best. He was at the top of his game and was making more money than he had ever imagined possible just for doing the thing he loved the most in the world. Could it get any better than that? Well, maybe one thing was missing, but Tony took steps to sort that out too. He asked Cindy to marry him.

Tony Hawk and Cindy Dunbar got married in the

backyard of their Fallbrook house beside the trampo-
line and the pool. It was a moving ceremony — except
according to Tony, the Justice of the Peace who married them kept calling him Andy. So much for fame.

And though Tony and Cindy were personally
happy, ominous signs for Tony's sport appeared on
the horizon. By the middle of 1990, it became evident
that all was not well in the world of skateboarding.
Tony knew something was up when his royalty
checks starting getting halved every other month.
Then the demos and the contests started drying up.
The NSA started losing money big time, and so did
the big skateboard companies like Powell. With their
huge facilities, their large staffs, and their big inven-
tories, they were terribly vulnerable to any downturn in
the popularity of skating.

Everybody on the front lines of skating saw the end
coming. How could you miss it? Tony went to Japan to
do a demo with Bucky Lasek and Lance Mountain.
Even the year before such a demo would have drawn
thousands of excited people. This time though, they
found themselves skating in front of an audience of 30.
And it wasn't just Japan. It was the same everywhere
they went. Skating was dying a quick, universal death.

For the newly married Tony Hawk, it meant watching his income do a nose dive. He went from making
more money than he knew what to do with to barely
eking out a living. The first year wasn't bad because of

money that was coming in from contracts, but even so, he went from making $150,000 in 1989 to $75,000 in 1990. Tony Hawk knew it was going to get a lot worse before it got any better.

Chapter Five

Even Tony Hawk couldn't imagine exactly how much worse it was going to get. Every month he watched as his royalties got cut further and further, until finally Cindy was making more as a manicurist than Tony was bringing in as a star skater. He and Cindy put themselves on a major budget, including limiting Tony to $5 a day for Taco Bell, his favorite fast food restaurant. Still, although Tony knew things were bad, he figured he could manage to buy his favorite car — a Lexus. Mind you, it was a *used* Lexus, and it "only" cost 30 grand. Some budget.

It wasn't only Tony who was in trouble. Powell & Peralta were losing in their intense competition with World Industries. They were just too big and too corporate to survive in the radical skateboarding world of 1991. Realizing that he was going to have to make a move sooner or later, Tony and fellow skater Per Welinder started planning to launch their own company. Capitalizing on Tony's recognition value and last name, they decided to call their new enterprise Birdhouse Industries.

The first thing they needed was money, and that was suddenly in short supply. Tony and Per decided to keep their plans secret while they worked up a business plan and figured out where they were going to find the cash to start their company. Tony took out a new mortgage on his Carlsbad house, then he looked around at what other things he had that could bring in some money. Tony finally realized that the Lexus was going to have to go. Although it broke his heart, he sold the car to Cindy's parents, bought a Honda Civic, and put the remaining money into the Birdhouse fund.

Meanwhile, Tony continued to compete in contests. He went to a contest in France and won there. Then he went on to Germany and won again. The crowds were getting smaller and smaller, but Tony had been through these downswings before and he knew that if he could just keep going long enough, things would eventually turn around again. While continuing to skate for Powell, Tony started putting together a team for Birdhouse. He quietly recruited a number of top, young skaters, including Jeremy Klein, Willy Santos, and Mike Frazier.

After winning yet another vert contest in Houston, and taking the NSA world champ award one more time, Tony finally decided it was time to make his move. He informed Powell & Peralta of his decision to leave. It was a difficult thing for him to do. Part of the difficulty was the uncertainty he was moving into. But even more than that was the sadness he felt at leaving the company that had sponsored him for so many years and that had been such a large part of his life. But everything changes sooner or later, and it was more and more clear to Tony that Powell was not going to survive the changes taking place in the skateboarding industry. If he needed any evidence that his judgement was right, he got it soon after he left when Stacy Peralta followed suit and departed the company he had helped found.

Starting the new company wasn't easy for Tony, though. The skateboard market was flooded with product at a time when almost no one was interested in buying. The first year of Birdhouse was even slower than Tony and Per had figured it would be. They were losing money like crazy. By March of 1992, Tony's income was barely enough to cover the mortgages on his two houses and the utility bills. Everything else had to be covered by Cindy's income.

And that, of course, is when Cindy got pregnant. Tony and Cindy couldn't have been happier. But their happiness was colored by their anxiety. A child meant more expenses, and more expenses was the last thing they needed right then. So they tightened their budget even more.

That summer, the Birdhouse team went on its first demo tour. It wasn't exactly a luxury tour. On the contrary, they traveled in an old, rented van and crammed everybody into one budget motel room wherever they were. With Tony now in charge of running the tour, things didn't go all that smoothly, either. Skaters have never been known for their organizational skills, and Tony was no exception to the rule. On top of everything else, half the dealers they did demos for ripped them off for their fee. By the time they got back to California, Birdhouse had lost $7,000 on the tour.

Still, it wasn't all a loss for Tony. Even though skating was on the skids, and even though he was on the brink of financial disaster, the tour had given him something he hadn't anticipated. Once again, he had gotten so far away from his roots that he'd lost touch with the joy of skating just for the fun of it. The tour forced him to remember exactly what skating was all about. Even if it cost Birdhouse seven grand, Tony figured it had been worth it.

In December, two things happened that deeply affected Tony's life. On December 6, Cindy gave birth to a baby boy. They decided to name him Hudson Riley Hawk, and call him Riley. Shortly after that, the National Skating Association, the organization that Frank Hawk had built and nurtured over the years, and that Tony had grown up with, finally died, pulled under by the death of skating itself. Often in life, Tony found, great joy and great sadness arrived together.

The popularity of skating continued to slide, and along with it the financial prospects of Birdhouse Enterprises. Suddenly, $5 a day for Taco Bell was too much, and Tony Hawk, the guy who had pulled in $150,000 less than two years before, found his allowance cut down to $2.50 a day. It was no wonder, then, that he started thinking about other career options. It didn't seem like skating was offering much hope.

One of the things Tony had been interested in for a while was film editing. If he couldn't make a living skating, he thought, maybe he could do it editing videos. With an $8,000 loan from his parents, Tony went to a used equipment store and managed to put together a workable editing system. Over the next several months he got work editing a couple of skate videos, but when he tallied up his earnings, he just wasn't making enough. He knew the situation called for drastic action. As much as it broke his heart to do it, he decided that he had to sell the Fallbrook house, and that he and Cindy would move back to Carlsbad.

It was a bleak time for Tony Hawk. And just when he thought it couldn't get any worse, it did. He put the Fallbrook house on the market, but nobody wanted to buy it. All the stress about money was starting to take its toll on his relationship with Cindy. Birdhouse was sinking. The kind of skating Tony did was now almost antique. Vert skating seemed to be dead. Tony Hawk began to feel that the world he had grown up in, the world that meant everything to him, the world of skating, no longer wanted anything to do with him.

His life was falling apart, and it all seemed to be symbolized by the ramp at the Fallbrook house that his father had built for him. It, too, was falling apart. The plywood was worn through in spots. It was so worn and weather-beaten that it had gotten really slow. It was crumbling away just like his life.

One day while Tony was out skating the ramp, wondering what he was going to do with his life, something happened. He flipped his board in a move that he had never thought he was capable of doing. Suddenly Tony's spirits started to pick up. He ran up the ramp and tried it again. Over and over he pushed himself to complete the move, until finally he got it. He swooped down the crumbling ramp, kicked a heelflip varial lien, caught the board and landed. Completing the new move made him realize that he wasn't over the hill, that this old dog could still learn new tricks.

It would have been nice if everything had turned around after that, but it never really works that way except in the movies. Tony's marriage continued to fall apart. Birdhouse still lost money. The Fallbrook house still didn't sell. But somehow, completing that trick made it all more bearable for Tony. There was still hope. That summer when the Birdhouse team went on tour, they didn't even have enough money to rent a van.

They had to borrow Cindy's minivan for the trip. But there was a sign that things were changing for the better — sort of. When they got back after the tour and totaled up their receipts, they had only lost $6,000 this time.

Both Tony and Per Welinder figured that, based on the previous cycles, skating should probably start picking up again in 1994. The question was, could they hang on long enough to see it. Birdhouse was almost dead and they were thinking seriously of taking it off life support. Tony, Birdhouse's biggest asset, was so tied up with other business that he wasn't getting to skate much. He had managed to work out some new vert tricks, but street skating was the only thing anybody was interested in, so nobody even cared what he was up to.

Finally, Tony decided that he had had enough. He retired. Again. At about the same time, the Fallbrook house finally sold and he had to tear down the ramp. Then in September, things came to head between Cindy and him. They realized that their marriage wasn't working and decided to separate. It was a friendly separation. Both of them agreed that they had grown apart and needed to figure out what to do next. They agreed to share custody of Riley. After a few months, they realized that they weren't going to get back together again and started divorce proceedings.

The only good news was that it was beginning to seem that 0Tony and Per were right about the state of the skateboarding business. They were starting to get more requests to do demos. It looked like maybe skating's popularity was picking up a bit.

One of those requests was for a show in Santa Rosa, California, that involved skateboarders, inline skaters, and BMXers. This was the beginning of the idea of so-called "extreme" sports, and the show was called "Extreme Wheels Live." The name itself was enough to make Tony think about taking a pass. But the fee was $3,000 and he had a mortgage payment coming up. When he accepted the offer, he had no idea how his life was about to change.

While he was checking in for the show, Tony noticed one of the other athletes, a cute rollerblader named Erin. Over the course of the show, they spent some time together and really hit it off. After the show was over, they went their separate ways but spent hours talking together on the phone. They started seeing each other, though not technically dating until Tony invited Erin to go to Santa Monica with him. After that, it got serious pretty quickly.

With skateboarding picking up again, Tony and Per thought Birdhouse should be doing better than it was. It still wasn't making the kind of money they had planned on. Finally they decided that what they needed was a famous skater competing on the company's team. They happened to know just the guy, too. So, Tony Hawk came out of retirement for the second time and went back on the contest circuit. Birdhouse reissued the Tony Hawk board and it quickly became the company's bestseller.

Their timing was perfect. "Extreme sport" was picking up steam like crazy. It had excited enormous interest, especially among young people. In 1995, the ESPN television network decided to cash in on the craze and organized the first televised *Extreme Games* in June. As much as Tony Hawk hated the name, he recognized a great opportunity when he saw it. For one thing, the games were going to feature ramp skating, and Tony hoped it would be a chance for his sport to reclaim its former popularity. For another, with millions of people watching, the games would offer skating more exposure than it ever had before.

Many people in the skating world were skeptical about the Extreme Games. They felt that it was a sellout of the integrity of their sport. Hardcore skaters never trusted outsiders' interest in skating, and with reason, too. Usually, outsiders misrepresented skating to serve their own purposes. Tony considered all the angles, and then finally decided that he couldn't *not* go. It was too great an opportunity to pass up, whatever the dangers might be.

The Extreme Games (or the X Games as they later became known) were a huge success. Millions of people watched Tony Hawk win first place in the vert event and second place in the street skating event.

Dubbed "The Michael Jordan of Skating," Tony quickly became a major celebrity in the U.S. He couldn't go out without being recognized. Suddenly, Birdhouse products took off like a rocket. The roller coaster had clearly bottomed out, but Tony Hawk was on his way up again, and this time, the ride promised to go higher than ever before.

For Tony, the moment was a mixed one. It was a relief to know that he wasn't going to wind up digging ditches for a living. But some terrible news had cast a shadow over his triumph. Frank Hawk, the man who had loved and supported Tony and done everything in his power to help him succeed at the sport he loved, had been diagnosed with terminal cancer. Tony wanted to spend as much time as possible with his father before he died, but Frank wouldn't hear of it. He insisted that his son carry on with his life, especially since Tony was at a crucial turning point in his skating career.

One of the great joys of those first X Games for Tony was knowing that his father was able to see him on TV in his moment of triumph. That summer, on tour with the Birdhouse Team, Tony got news of his father's death. He returned home for the funeral. Frank was cremated and Tony and Steve scattered Frank's ashes in the Pacific Ocean — all except for a little bit they held back to take to Home Depot.

Tony's life over the next few years just kept getting better and better. Financially, Birdhouse couldn't have been in stronger shape. The Airwalk shoe company came out with a Tony Hawk shoe that netted him $38,000 in royalties the first year. When Birdhouse went on tour in 1997, it wasn't in a rented van with overnights in cheap motels. This time they rented a huge RV that was stocked with a bar, a Play Station, and a VCR, and hired someone to drive the thing. At night they stayed in nice hotels, and everybody got their own room.

The other thing Tony wanted was a ramp he could call his own. Ever since he had sold the Fallbrook house and torn down the ramp his father had built for him, he had been skating at the YMCA near Carlsbad. It wasn't bad, but it wasn't like having your own ramp, either. The hours it was open were limited, for one thing, and he couldn't always get all the time he needed. So he found a warehouse in Irvine and had a 48-foot (14.6-m) wide ramp built in it. The ramp had 10.5-foot (3.2-m) transitions and 1.5 feet (43 cm) of vert. It was a deal, too. It only cost $15,000, all of which could be written off Tony's taxes.

Once Tony realized that Erin and his son, Riley, were going to get along with each other, that relationship moved ahead too. At the end of 1995, Tony and Erin moved in together. As he spent more and more time on the road, she began to spend more and more time caring for Riley. Tony realized that he wanted to spend the rest of his life with Erin, and started looking for a way ask her to marry him.

He finally hit on a solution. Knowing that she was looking at houses, Tony decided to surprise her. Erin particularly liked one house she had looked at in Carlsbad, so Tony secretly bought it. He also bought a ring. Then one night he took her out to the house where he proposed to her. They tied the knot on September 28, 1996, and honeymooned in Hawaii.

By 1997, the popularity of skating was out of control. No one could have predicted how much interest the X Games were going to generate. It was wild. Suddenly Tony Hawk found that he was overbooked. He couldn't keep up with all the requests for demos and appearances, not to mention product endorsements. He finally gave up trying to do it himself and hired his sister Pat as his manager. She eventually talked him into hiring a publicist — someone who would organize Tony's public appearances and handle his interviews with the media. Eventually Tony would become the only skater in the U.S. who had both a manager and a publicist.

By the time the third X Games competition rolled around in 1997, the skating community was totally divided. On the one hand, the Games had increased people's knowledge of skating. That, in turn, had improved its image and increased its popularity to the point where, for the first time, skaters could make real money competing. As a lot of skaters feared, however, TV also misrepresented skating. Announcers who knew nothing of skate history or skate culture were suddenly experts and were repeating to millions of viewers stuff that just wasn't true. A lot of skaters were disgusted.

Tony Hawk found himself caught in between. His name was now tied to the X Games. Millions of Americans thought of him when they thought of skating. And when they thought of him, they thought of the X Games. Almost without choosing, Tony became a kind of middleman, trying to sort out the differences between skaters and the X Games organizers.

The 1997 Games were held in San Diego, Tony's home town. That put a lot of pressure on him. The year before he had only placed second in the vert contest, losing out to his friend Andy Macdonald. Tony's whole family would be there watching him in San Diego, and he wanted to win it for them. After watching Rune Glifberg do a fabulous run, Tony did one of his best runs ever in a competition. Knowing he had taken first, he spent the rest of his time trying to pull off the elusive 9, but he couldn't do it.

The popularity of skating and Tony's success as a skater led to another big opportunity for him. He had always been something of a computer geek. In 1998

Activision, a video game developer, came to him and proposed making a skate game for Game Boy. Tony was excited about the idea and threw himself into the project. The rest is history. Tony worked with Activision to produce "Tony Hawk's Pro Skater" for Game Boy. It became one of the best-selling games of all time, followed up by "Proskater Two".

With Birdhouse now the most popular and successful skate company in the world, Tony figured it was time to make his own skate video. He hoped it would help set Birdhouse apart from other skate companies. It was also the chance to have a really good time with the Birdhouse team. One hundred and sixty thousand dollars later, Birdhouse had produced *The End*, a major skate movie shot entirely on film, not videotape. It involved building a ramp in a bullring in Mexico, blowing up some cars, and burning down part of the Birdhouse warehouse (accidentally). The video was a huge success. When it premiered on October 8, 1998, at the Galaxy in Santa Ana, California, the showing concluded with a small riot provoked by overly aggressive bouncers and nervous police.

The year 1999 started off great for Tony. On March 28, Tony and Erin welcomed Spencer Hawk into the world. Riley now had a brother! And Tony continued to win contests, even though a lot of people thought that at age 31, he was over the hill. If there was a downside to all that success, it was only that after a while he started to burn out, even with a publicist and a manager. For Tony, skating had always been about having fun. And he realized at the beginning of 1999 that the contests weren't fun anymore.

It wasn't like the two other times he'd retired. He wasn't depressed or freaked out about the state of skating this time. He just didn't want to do it anymore. Of course skating, which is so unlike other sports in many ways, is unlike them in retirement, too. When you retire from football, you stop playing football. But retiring in skating just means no more contests. The skating still goes on and on.

"I might as well have been digging a ditch," Tony said later. Feeling that way, he knew there was only one thing for him to do.

Pulling off the 9 at the 1999 summer X Games was the sign Tony needed. He'd been after that trick for years. It was the last trick on the list he'd made decades before. So when he succeeded, he knew it was time to retire for good. That summer at the Triple Crown Finals in Huntington Beach, he told a local reporter the news. And that was that.

Except, of course, it wasn't, not for the guy who'd already retired twice. After he publicly retired for the third time, he remembered he had committed to do an event in Las Vegas for MTV. But for real, after that, no more contests.

Since the MTV event, Tony has been busy. He signed with the ESPN sports channel to be a commentator for skate contests. He's working on two more video games, and he is thinking about producing another Birdhouse skate video. There is a line of Tony Hawk clothing. On top of all that, he's still busy doing skate demos. In June of 2000, Tony Hawk's Gigantic Skatepark Tour rolled across the U.S. carrying the message of skating to another generation of America's youth. The opportunities seem endless for the scrawny kid from Oceanside, California, who got expelled from nursery school. Skateboarding is now riding the largest wave of popularity in its history. And Tony Hawk is still out there on the edge, hanging ten.

Glossary of Skateboarding Terms

180: (pronounced "one-eighty") a one-hundred-and-eighty-degree turn, or half a circle; a measure of rotation. Used to describe skateboarding tricks, e.g., the 180 frontside ollie.

360: (pronounced "three-sixty") a three-hundred-and-sixty-degree rotation (a full circle). Used to describe skateboarding tricks, e.g., a 360 shove-it kickflip.

Air: riding a skateboard into the air while holding it with the intention of landing and continuing the ride. From "aerial."

Backside: the direction of a turn on an incline, meaning the backside of the body is facing the wall; the opposite of *frontside*.

Blunt: going up over an object and landing with the

tail along the edge of the object and the rear two wheels on top of the object. The board should then be pointing in a near vertical position.

Deck: main platform area of a skateboard.

Fakie: a word used to signify the skater is going backwards. The skater's board moves backwards while the skater stands in his standard position. Not to be confused with *opposite-footed*.

Fat: meaning "high" or "far." Used to express a skateboarding trick that is performed over a long distance or to a great height. Also spelled *phat*.

Flatland: type of street skating that became popular in the late 80s and early 90s that involved tricks done on flat ground, usually things like kickflips, pressure flips, etc.

Flip: a move developed from freestyle skating. It involves making your board turn upside down in a variation of combinations; generally, when the board completely flips over and lands back on the wheels.

Freestyle: an type of skating that has now become part of street and vert skating. Used to be performed on low-riding skinny boards. Tricks consisted of numerous balancing moves, flips and shove-its.

Frontside: generally refers to the direction of a turn on an incline when the front of the body is facing the wall. The opposite of *backside*.

Goofy: when you skate with your right foot forward. The opposite of *regular*.

Grind: a trick done on any sharp lip where the truck comes in contact with the edge of the pool, curb, ramp, etc. The act of performing said trick, e.g., to *grind* a rail.

Handplant: a form of handstand where your board is held in the air either by a hand or feet.

Kickturn: rotating on the rear wheels of the board with the front wheels raised from the surface.

Nose: the part of the deck in front of the front truck. Opposite end to the *tail*.

Nosegrab: grabbing the front of the board (*nose*) with the leading hand.

Nosegrind: grinding on the leading truck only.

Noseslide: sliding along an object using the underside of the nose.

Ollie: a move invented on ramps by Alan "Ollie" Gelfand and brought to the streets by Rodney Mullen. An air without using your hands; the basis for most skateboarding tricks.

Regular: you skate regular if you skate with your left foot forward. The opposite is *goofy*!

Revert: finishing a trick coming out forwards, then quickly sliding round 180 to come out backwards.

Shuffle: an extra element to add to a trick by landing sideways, or with the wheels parallel to the lip, and then sliding the wheels to reenter backwards. To do a backside air shuffle, do the motion for a backside air, but as you reenter, land sideways with the wheels just below the coping and slide to a fakie position.

Shove-it or **Shuv-it:** turning the board without turning your body so the board spins round under your feet.

Slalom: similar to the back-and-forth motion used by

downhill skiers, except on hard ground, usually using a dedicated skateboard.

Slam: basically another word for falling off your board and hurting yourself.

Slappy: doing grinds along such things as a curb without ollie-ing onto it.

Stance: either *regular* or *goofy*. The way you stand on your board.

Street Skating: refers to any skating that is done using only those objects or obstacles found in the urban environment. Examples: fire hydrants, school-yards, curbs, stairs, handrails. Also often refers to the simulated smaller ramps and banks found in "street courses" at skateparks.

Tail: the part of the deck behind the rear truck. Opposite end to the *nose*.

Technical: name given to complex skating, i.e. freestyle. Involves flipping and shove-it-ing your board in all manner of directions.

Truck: device that fixes to the bottom of the board,

and holds the wheels in place. Two are needed (a pair) per skateboard. A complete truck is made up of a baseplate, hanger, axle, kingpin, cushions, two special washers and two bolts for the axles.

Vert: part of an inclined surface that is vertical in gradient.

Wallie: skating onto, up, and over a street object.

Wheelside: technique of slowing down without putting your feet down. It is what people may commonly call a skid.

Some Basic Skateboarding Moves

Skaters are constantly inventing new moves. Each decade in the last 50 years has had its characteristic tricks. Some moves, such as the ollie, redefined skating and became the basis of many of the moves that follow. The names are highly inventive as well. Sometimes they are purely descriptive, as with the kickflip, the 900, or the Rock 'n' Roll. Sometimes the moves are named after the skater who first invented them, like the ollie and the cab. Sometimes, people just make up names because they sound good.

It's almost impossible to describe skateboard moves in print. You really have to see them to know them. Here are some moves to watch for on your favorite skate video:

Backside varial kickflip: The varial kickflip is a combination of the backside pop shove-it and the ollie kickflip. As you go into the air, the board does a 180 under you, while it also flips.

Fakie ollie: With the ollie to tail you are moving backwards and popping the tail. The tail needs to pop really fast so the board doesn't stop. There are endless variations of the fakie ollie, like the fakie ollie to tail, backside fakie 180 ollie (also known as a half cab), etc.

Frontside pop shove-it: The frontside pop shove-it is a trick that can be done small and quick (best for learning) or big and high. To do the trick, you ollie, pushing the tail so that the board does a frontside 180, while your body remains facing the same way.

Half-cab: The backside half-cab is a street version of the vert trick of the same name. It is a backside fakie 180 ollie. The original Cabalaerial, invented by the legendary Steve Caballero, is a vert move in which the rider fakies up the wall, pops a 360 ollie, and comes down forward. The half-cab is the same thing, but the skater only pops a 180 ollie, he fakies up the wall, and fakies down the wall.

No-comply: The no-comply has gone by a few different names, including the "no-handed boneless," and the "step-hop." It involves putting one foot on the ground, then jumping back onto the deck. By popping the tail harder and jumping more, you can go higher.

Nollie: The Nollie is an ollie done off the nose. You roll forward, and pop the nose on the ground to get in the air.

Ollie: One of the fundamental moves of contemporary skating. Start by riding forward, with your rear foot on the tail and your front foot about midway up the board. You jump, while slapping the tail into the ground with a good strong pop. Because you are jumping, and your weight is off the board, the pop will cause the board to bounce into the air. At this point, the front foot begins to drag up toward the nose, moving forward. This will level the board out in the air. You also use it to "drag" the board up with you as you jump, which increases the altitude of your ollie.

Ollie kickflip: Take off in an ollie with a nice pop, dragging your front foot up the board. Use the front foot to flick the board into a flip. As you drag your foot up the board, you flick your foot to your heel side, which is what makes the flip happen. Continue the flick as your front foot kicks out in front and to the side. Stay right above the board and come back to the correct landing position after flicking it.

Rock 'n' roll: a very basic move for vert, mini-ramp,

and ditch skating. It involves riding to the top of the wall, hanging your front wheels over the edge, rocking on the bottom of your board, and then kick turning back in.

Varial kickflip: a combination of the backside pop shove-it and the ollie kickflip. The board does a 180 under you, while it also flips.

Research Sources

Borden, Iain. "Urban Space and Representation."
http://www.noottingham.ac.uk/3cities/textbord.htm

Brooke, Michael. *The Concrete Wave*. Toronto:
Warwick, 1999.

"Chairman of the Board."
http://www.sikids.com/shorter/video/hawk/in
dex.html (Quicktime movies of Tony Hawk's
greatest tricks)

Davis, James. *Skateboard Roadmap*. NY: Carlton, 1999.

Hawk, Tony, and Sean Mortimer. *Hawk, Occupation:
Skateboarder*. New York: Regan Books, 2000.

CHAMPION SPORT
BIOGRAPHIES

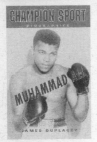

CHECK OUT THE OTHER TITLES IN THE SERIES!